The Story of Flight

MODERN MILITARY AIRCRAFT

Crabtree Publishing Company
www.crabtreebooks.com

PMB 16A, 350 Fifth Avenue,
Suite 3308
New York, NY 10118

612 Welland Avenue
St. Catharines, Ontario
L2M 5V6

Published in 2003 by
Crabtree Publishing Company

Coordinating editor: Ellen Rodger
Project editors: Sean Charlebois, Carrie Gleason
Production coordinator: Rose Gowsell

Created and Produced by
David West Children's Books

Project Development, Design, and Concept
David West Children's Books:
Designer: Rob Shone
Editor: James Pickering
Illustrators: James Field & Ross Watton (SGA),
Gary Slater & Steve Weston (Specs Art),
Colin Howard (Advocate), Alex Pang
Picture Research: Carlotta Cooper

Photo Credits:
Abbreviations: t-top, m-middle, b-bottom, r-right,
l-left, c-center.

Front cover tm & pages 11mr, 4tr, 11tr, 12tl, 14tl,
17tr, 26b - Rex features Ltd. 5tr, 9br, 20br, 22bl -
Corbis Images. 6tl, 8tl, 16bm, 20tl, 23tr, 25tr, 29tr -
The Flight Collection. 7mr - Hulton Archive. 13mr
(PC 94/201/586), 14bl (PC 75/2/6030) - Royal Air
Force Museum. 16tl, 19tr, 22tl, 25bl, 26tl, 27tr,
28tl - BAE Systems 2000.

06 05 04 03
10 9 8 7 6 5 4 3 2 1

Cataloging in Publication Data
Hansen, Ole Steen.
    Modern military aircraft / Ole Steen Hansen.
        p. cm. -- (The story of flight)
Includes index.
ISBN 0-7787-1204-4 (RLB) -- ISBN 0-7787-1220-6 (PB)
    1. Airplanes, Military--Juvenile literature. [1. Airplanes, Military.]
I. Title.
    UG1240.H357 2003
    623.7'46--dc21
                                2002156481
                                LC

The Story of Flight

MODERN MILITARY AIRCRAFT

Ole Steen Hansen

Crabtree Publishing Company
www.crabtreebooks.com

CONTENTS

BERLIN AIRLIFT
After World War II ended, the city of Berlin, Germany's capital, was divided in half. The Soviet Union controlled one half and cut off transportation routes. Hundreds of American transport aircraft flew in supplies of food and fuel.

FASTER THAN SOUND
In 1947, American pilot Chuck Yeager flew the rocket powered X-1 plane faster than the speed of sound. Soon after, combat jets were designed to be supersonic.

INTRODUCTION

The Cold War lasted from the end of World War II in 1945 to the early 1990s. The term Cold War refers not to an actual war, but to a period of time when the world's major powers, the United States and the Soviet Union, mistrusted each other and assumed the other country would attack. Many countries around the world sided with either of these two superpowers. The Cold War was not fought by soldiers on the ground. It was a war based on which country could produce the most powerful weapons. Aircraft and missiles became the most dangerous weapons of the Cold War. The dreaded Third World War never came, but smaller wars were fought in countries around the world.

F-18 FORMATION FLYING
Modern jets, such as the F-18, are aircraft that can fly as bombers, fighters, or reconnaissance aircraft. The U.S. Navy Blue Angels formation teams fly them at air shows too!

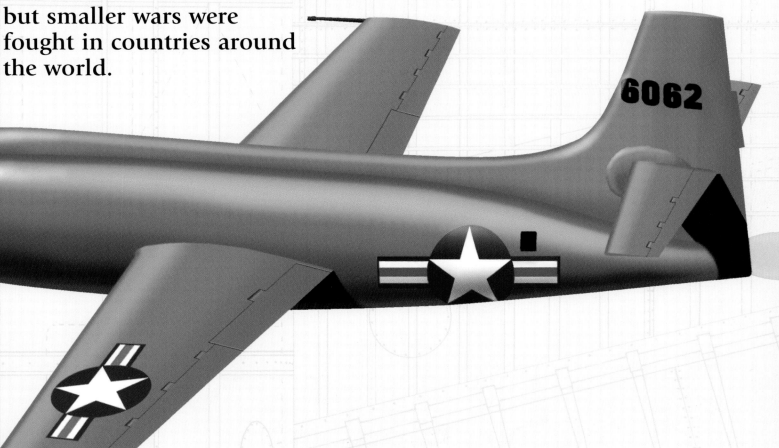

6062

KOREA

In 1950, communist **North Korea attacked** South Korea. It was a Cold War clash between communist and democratic countries. Unfortunately for the Korean people, their country became a battlefield as soldiers and aircraft from many countries came to fight in their small Far-Eastern nation.

GRUMMAN F9F PANTHER
The Panther was the most used U.S. Navy jet when the Korean War began. When a Panther destroyed a Russian-built YAK-9 it became the first naval jet to shoot down an enemy plane.

Most aircraft fighting over Korea were **piston-engined** aircraft from World War II, such as the B-29 Superfortress bombers that had been used to attack Japan. P-51 Mustangs **strafed** ground targets with rockets, bombs, and the chemical napalm. The communist side even used old PO-2 biplanes that had been used during World War II.

PO-2 aircraft were used as nighttime bombers because they were light and quiet. Faster night fighters could not fly slow enough to shoot down the PO-2s. During the Korean War, jet aircraft fought each other for the first time. Early jets, such as the American F-86 and the Russian MiG-15, were not very different from World War II fighters, except they had **jet engines** and swept-back wings. These early jets were not supersonic, had no radar, and were not armed with missiles.

JET VERSUS JET

In Korea, American pilots flying F-86 Sabre jets were much more experienced than pilots flying MiG-15s. These early jets had guns to shoot down enemy planes, but at high speed the guns were very difficult to use. Each air force realized that they had to develop missiles for jet-to-jet combat.

Helicopters in War

During the Korean War, large numbers of helicopters were used for the first time. Thousands of wounded soldiers were rescued from the battlefield by speedy helicopters and taken straight to the hospital, often less than an hour after being injured.

TA-183

The combat jets of the Korean War owed a lot to German **aerodynamic** research done during World War II. At first, the American F-86 Sabre was designed with straight wings. Captured German documents made it clear that the jet would be much faster with swept-back wings. The German Focke-Wulf Ta-183 fighter jet was built, but not flown, before World War II ended, and was taken to the Soviet Union. The Russians were very impressed with the design and based the MiG-15 jet on it.

THE NUCLEAR THREAT

During the Cold War, people in the Western democracies and the communist regimes in Eastern Europe lived under the threat of being completely wiped out by nuclear bombs. **Each side wanted to prevent the other side from attacking.**

VULCAN

Britain's Royal Air Force used the four-engined Avro Vulcan bomber to keep up the nuclear threat. These big delta-winged bombers were always ready to take off with a few minutes' warning.

The logic behind this terrible threat was called MAD, which means "mutually assured destruction." The first country to attack using nuclear weapons would be destroyed by the other country's weapons. During the early years of the Cold War, the U.S. Air Force relied on the huge bombers of its Strategic Air Command (SAC) to deliver the nuclear bombs. The motto of SAC was "peace is our profession," but it was by preparing for nuclear war that they were able to secure peace.

U.S. AIR FORCE

TUPOLEV Tu-16

The Tupolev Tu-16 "Badger" long range bomber was first flown in 1952, and 1,509 were built. Production ended in 1963, but the Tu-16 served throughout the Cold War with the Soviet Air Force. It was used for reconnaissance, as a spy plane, and could carry nuclear bombs. Later versions of the aircraft carried cruise missiles, which are low-flying missiles that can avoid obstacles in their path, to hit land or sea targets.

NOISE AND SMOKE

The most important U.S. nuclear bomber was the mighty eight-engined Boeing B-52. The design of the swept-back wings and the engine location were based on German aerodynamic research during World War II.

The first U.S. bomber capable of hitting targets in the Soviet Union was the Convair B-36 "Peacemaker," powered by six piston engines and four jet engines. Later aircraft such as the B-52 and the supersonic B-58 "Hustler" were used. The air forces of the Soviet Union, France, and Britain also built jets that could carry nuclear weapons. Later, the United States and the Soviet Union developed nuclear missiles. The nuclear forces were always ready to go into action with little warning. Fortunately, the big nuclear bang never came. Perhaps they realized after all that, MAD made it completely mad to go to war!

Nuclear Nerve Center

For decades, the MAD nuclear threat meant thousands of people were employed in radar stations, control centers, and missile and bomber bases. If the dreaded "blips" appeared on the radar screens, there would only have been a very short time to find out if the threat was real, and how to strike back.

LOCKHEED U-2

The Lockheed U-2 jet was first flown in 1955. It had very long wings and was difficult to fly. It could fly too high for Soviet guns and fighters to hit it. Amazingly, the U-2S, a later version of the U-2, is still in service with the U.S. Air Force. The U-2S is used for reconnaissance against **terrorists** and countries that are considered enemies of the United States. This reconnaissance aircraft is also used to help in areas suffering from floods, earthquakes, and forest fires.

BLACKBIRD

The 1964 Lockheed SR 71 Blackbird flew at three times the speed of sound, 100,000 feet (30,000 m) above sea level. It could look deep into hostile airspace without actually flying over it.

SPY FLIGHTS

During the Cold War, a secret war was fought using spy planes. The United States wanted information on how many aircraft, missiles, and weapons the Soviet Union had. In the 1950s and early 1960s, the only way to get this information was to fly over the Soviet Union.

Four-engined Boeing RB-50Gs, jam-packed with antennas and electronic equipment flew along the borders of the Soviet Union to find out where Soviet radar was located. Other aircraft flew to take photographs, or to study what the targets would look like on their radar screens if war broke out. The Soviet Union fired at these spy planes. Some spy planes were shot down, but the flights and losses were kept secret. Most of the spy planes flew so high that neither Soviet guns nor fighter jets could reach them. The Soviets did not complain about the flights, because they did not want to admit that they could not stop them. The United States also kept them secret because they did not want to admit to spying.

A HELPING HAND
Britain's Royal Air Force spied over the Soviet Union in the 1950s using RB-45 jets from the U.S. Air Force. The U.S. government would not allow these flights, so the RAF flew them. The RB-45 above stands with some of the cameras it could carry.

Gary Powers
Eventually, the Soviet Union developed anti-aircraft missiles to shoot down U-2 jets. U.S. spy pilot Gary Powers was shot down in his U-2 in 1960. Powers was captured by the Soviets and sentenced to ten years in prison with hard labor. After less than two years he was released in exchange for a Soviet spy.

INTERCEPTORS

Fighter planes designed to fly out, find, and stop attacking enemy aircraft are called interceptors. In the early 1950s, the first supersonic interceptors were made to try and stop jet-powered nuclear bombers. Air-to-air missiles were also developed at this time for shooting down enemies in open air combat.

COLD WAR ALERT

Radar had become essential for air defense during World War II. During the Cold War, both the Soviet Union and the United States expected air raids to be flown over the North Pole, because this was the shortest route between the two countries. The U.S. radar at Thule, Greenland was meant to spot approaching enemy aircraft.

In 1954, the F-104 Starfighter was built with a long needle-shaped fuselage, or body, and almost razor-sharp short wings. Everything in the design of the aircraft was meant to make it fly fast – and it did, at Mach 2, or twice the speed of sound. The French Mirage III, which flew in 1956, was the first European aircraft capable of flying at Mach 2.

LOCKHEED F-104 STARFIGHTER

Country: USA
Length: 54 ft 9 in (16.7 m)
Wingspan: 21 ft 11 in (6.7 m)
Speed: 1,320 mph (2,124 km/h)
Climb rate: 50,000 ft/min (15,250 m/min)

DASSAULT-BREGUET MIRAGE III

Country: France
Length: 50 ft 10 in (15.5 m)
Wingspan: 27 ft (8.2 m)
Speed: 1,460 mph (2,350 km/h)
Climb rate: 16,400 ft/min (5,000 m/min)

The English Electric Lightning from 1957 was the British Mach 2 interceptor. The Soviet MiG-21 was developed in the late 1950s, and the MiG is still being improved in new versions. More MiGs have been built than any other jet. Over 10,000 have been produced and they have been exported to 56 countries.

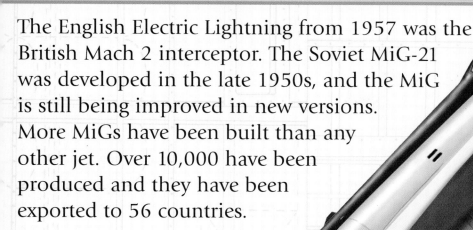

BAC (ENGLISH ELECTRIC) LIGHTNING
Country: Britain
Length: 55 ft 3 in (16.8 m)
Wingspan: 34 ft 10 in (10.6 m)
Speed: 1,500 mph (2,415 km/h)
Climb rate: 50,000 ft/min (15,250 m/min)

Sidewinders
Sidewinder heat-seeking missiles track their target by **homing in** on the hot exhaust from a plane's engines. Other missiles are controlled by radar, which is either in the missile itself or in the fighter firing it. Homing missiles are no guarantee of a hit because fighter pilots are constantly finding ways to avoid being hit.

MIKOYAN MiG-21
Country: USSR
Length: 44 ft 2 in (13.5 m)
Wingspan: 23 ft 5 in (7.2 m)
Speed: 1,386 mph (2,230 km/h)
Climb rate: 36,000 ft/min (11,000 m/min)

AFTERBURNERS
By burning fuel in the exhaust, an afterburner provides extra thrust, but the jet's fuel is used up at a very fast rate. Afterburners are therefore only used when necessary, but a few seconds' more power can be life saving in a combat situation.

Extra fuel burns, increasing thrust

Variable pitch nozzle

Fuel injected into exhaust

Hot exhaust gases

VIETNAM

During the war in Vietnam (1963–75), a large number of American aircraft of all sizes and types were used to support South Vietnam in the fight against communist troops from North Vietnam.

PITSTOP IN THE SKY

Vietnam was the first war in which in-flight refueling was used. American fighter bombers needed refueling in the air for their long missions. American tankers made 813,378 in-flight refuelings of aircraft during the war.

F-4 PHANTOM

Phantoms were the world's best multi-role fighters in the 1960s. Phantoms were flown in all kinds of missions over Vietnam. They supported ground forces in the South with bombs, rockets, and napalm. They also fought Russian-built MiGs over North Vietnam.

Parts of Vietnam were heavily bombed during the Vietnam War. The jungle was sprayed with chemicals to kill the trees and plants and show enemy hiding places in the forests. Over North Vietnam, powerful American Phantom fighter jets fought smaller, older, Russian-built MiGs flown by the North Vietnamese Air Force. Homing missiles launched from another aircraft or the ground could be outmaneuvered by pilots flying Phantoms.

Jungle Mission

In Vietnam, helicopters took American troops to fight North Vietnamese troops in the jungles, and evacuated the wounded. Heavily armed, they were also flown as "gun ships," protecting other helicopters. Thanks to helicopters, the U.S. forces in Vietnam could move around faster than any other army before. Helicopters were sometimes shot down by ground fire, and 2,382 were destroyed by the enemy. An equal number were lost in accidents.

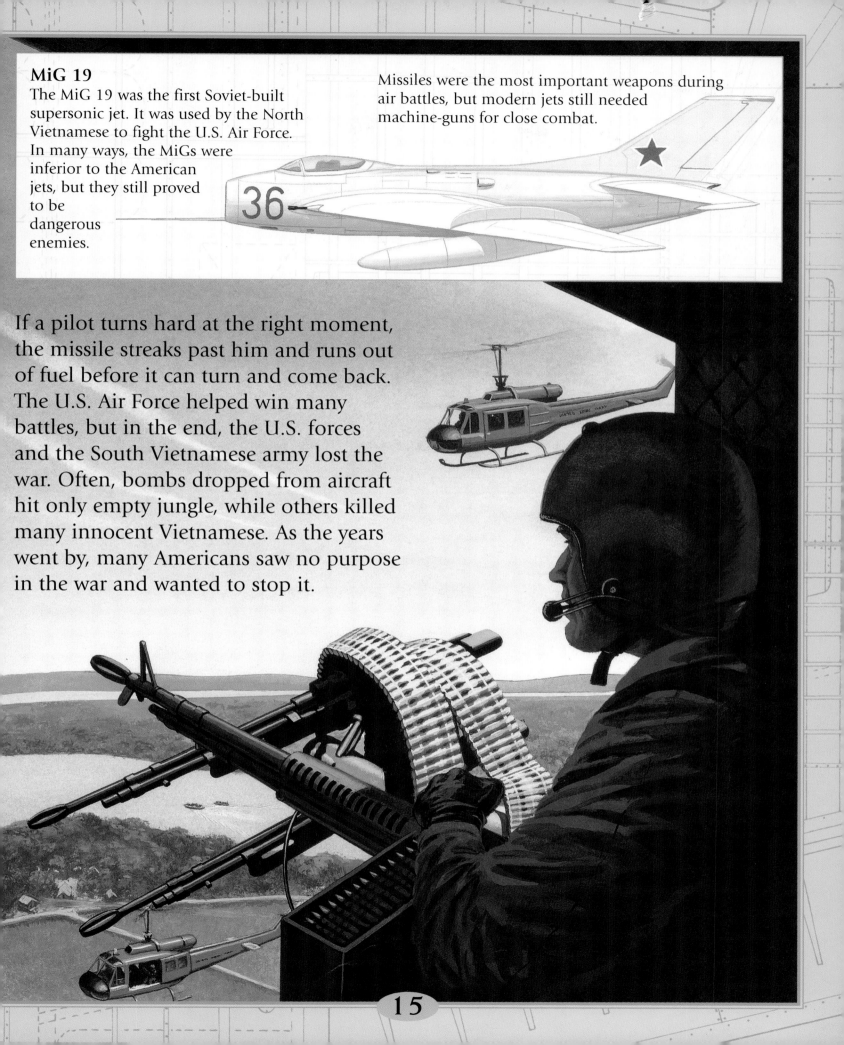

MiG 19

The MiG 19 was the first Soviet-built supersonic jet. It was used by the North Vietnamese to fight the U.S. Air Force. In many ways, the MiGs were inferior to the American jets, but they still proved to be dangerous enemies.

Missiles were the most important weapons during air battles, but modern jets still needed machine-guns for close combat.

If a pilot turns hard at the right moment, the missile streaks past him and runs out of fuel before it can turn and come back. The U.S. Air Force helped win many battles, but in the end, the U.S. forces and the South Vietnamese army lost the war. Often, bombs dropped from aircraft hit only empty jungle, while others killed many innocent Vietnamese. As the years went by, many Americans saw no purpose in the war and wanted to stop it.

NEW GENERATION FIGHTERS

In the 1970s and 1980s, a new generation of fighter jets were built that had more powerful engines. High speed was not as important as the fact that they could turn much quicker than older types of aircraft. Older jets, such as the Starfighter and Phantom, lost speed and altitude when they were turned quickly. The new fighters were also equipped with radar and all kinds of devices for self-defense.

SMART HELMETS

A fighter pilot has a helmet made to make sure it fits perfectly. The latest helmets have aiming devices that are linked to the aircraft's radar or missiles.

Today, fighters fire flares to fool heat seeking missiles. Instead of going for the engine, the missile explodes near the hot flare. Fighter jets can also shoot out thin strips of metal called chaff.

Things To Avoid

Modern fighter pilots have to avoid far more threats than jet fighters three or four decades ago. The British Rapier missile system is a very accurate short range missile. Other missiles, such as the Stinger, can be launched from the shoulder of a soldier. They can easily be moved, making it impossible for attacking aircraft to pinpoint the launch site.

McDONNELL DOUGLAS F-15 EAGLE
Country: USA
Length: 63 ft 9 in (19.4 m)
Wingspan: 42 ft 9 in (13 m)
Speed: 1,676 mph (2,698 km/h)

SUKHOI SU-27 "FLANKER"
Country: USSR
Length: 71 ft 2 in (21.9 m)

Wingspan: 47 ft 9 in (14.7 m)
Speed: 1,425 mph (2,280 km/h)

Hopefully, a radar-controlled missile will be "confused" and explode among the chaff instead of near the aircraft. A **radar warning receiver** tells the pilot if an enemy radar has found his aircraft. With a device called a jammer, the pilot then disturbs the enemy's radar. The enemy will know that an aircraft is jamming the radar, but not exactly where that aircraft is.

GENERAL DYNAMICS F-16 FIGHTING FALCON
Country: USA
Length: 47 ft 7 in (14.5 m)
Wingspan: 31 ft (9.5 m)
Speed: 1,333 mph (2,145 km/h)

PULLING Gs
Modern fighters turn so hard that the pilot has to endure 9G, which means that during the turn his body will feel nine times heavier. A tight-fitting g-suit stops the pilot from passing out.

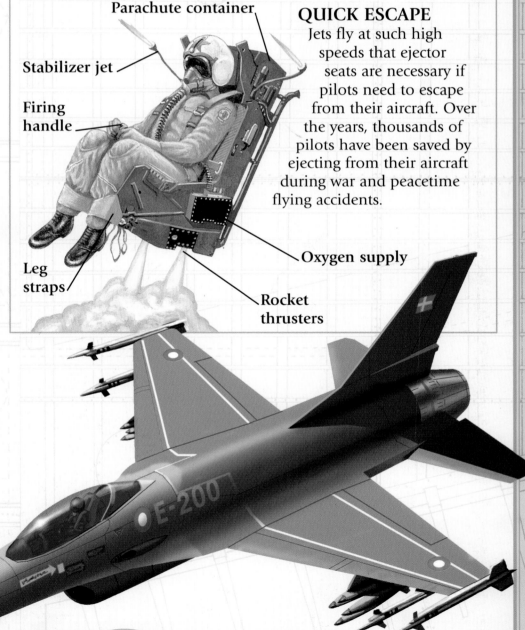

Parachute container

Stabilizer jet

Firing handle

Leg straps

QUICK ESCAPE
Jets fly at such high speeds that ejector seats are necessary if pilots need to escape from their aircraft. Over the years, thousands of pilots have been saved by ejecting from their aircraft during war and peacetime flying accidents.

Oxygen supply

Rocket thrusters

FAST AND LOW
The Tornado bomber is equipped with a terrain-following radar that makes it possible to fly low at supersonic speed at night or in bad weather.

SWING WINGS
The Tornado bomber has swing wings, also known as variable geometry wings. In the fully forward position, the wings provide plenty of lift. This is useful for take-off, landing, and turning quickly. Fully swept back, the wings are ideal for fast, low flying because they allow the plane to fly well through the turbulence that would otherwise give pilots a very bumpy ride, especially at low level.

Lever mechanism

Wing pivot

Minimum sweep

Maximum sweep

LOW LEVEL ATTACK

Over North Vietnam in the early 1970s, it became clear that the day of the high-flying big bomber was over. Against radar and missile defenses, bombers such as the B-52 were shot down. Bombers were built to be faster and smaller, like fighter jets.

In 1973, the Yom Kippur War broke out between Israel and neighboring Arab countries. Israeli fighter bombers were met by a highly developed Arab air defense, which used missiles and radars. The Israeli Air Force suffered heavy losses. During the Yom Kippur War, modern air defenses made it difficult for attacking aircraft to stay in the air. As a result, aircraft that could fly as low as possible were built. These were fast bombers which could hide in valleys and behind hills or woods, then wind their way close to the ground, toward their target. Flying low meant that air defenses had very little time to discover and react to an attacking bomber. The bombers also needed chaff, flares, radar warning receivers, and jammers, like the fighters.

HARRIERS
The Harrier fighter bomber can land and take-off vertically, so it can land almost everywhere. It can hide in a forest near the battle, attack quickly, and fly back into hiding.

AH-64 Apache

The Apache is an American attack helicopter that was developed after the Vietnam War. The crew is protected by a number of electronic devices and lightweight armor shields in the cockpit floor and sides. Designed to attack from low level, the Apache hides in the terrain on its way to its target. This heavily-armed helicopter is equipped to fly day and night, and in all kinds of weather.

THE GULF WAR

The 1991 Gulf War was won from the air. The Iraqi Air Force was the sixth largest in the world, but it was completely outclassed by the United States, British, French, and other air forces.

STEALTH BOMBER

The F-117 Night Hawk is designed to be impossible to see on radar. Flying at night, F-117 jets were used in the Gulf War to hit key targets with bombs.

AWACS

The Boeing E-3 Sentry AWACS (Airborne Warning and Control System) aircraft was developed during the Cold War to find low-flying bombers with its huge radar. During the Gulf War, AWACS aircraft kept track of all aircraft movement. A typical AWACS mission lasted between 16 and 18 hours. AWACS directed and controlled more than 3,000 combat **sorties** per day. These big, unarmed aircraft were the key to winning the air battle.

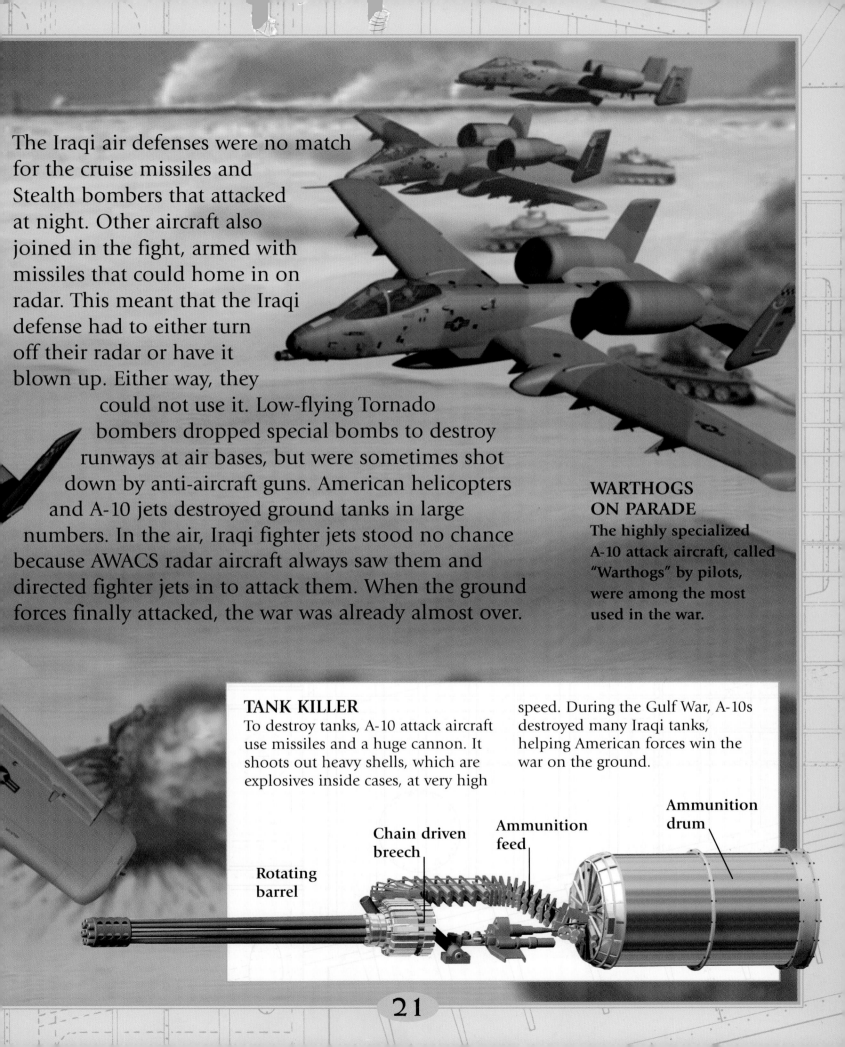

The Iraqi air defenses were no match for the cruise missiles and Stealth bombers that attacked at night. Other aircraft also joined in the fight, armed with missiles that could home in on radar. This meant that the Iraqi defense had to either turn off their radar or have it blown up. Either way, they could not use it. Low-flying Tornado bombers dropped special bombs to destroy runways at air bases, but were sometimes shot down by anti-aircraft guns. American helicopters and A-10 jets destroyed ground tanks in large numbers. In the air, Iraqi fighter jets stood no chance because AWACS radar aircraft always saw them and directed fighter jets in to attack them. When the ground forces finally attacked, the war was already almost over.

WARTHOGS ON PARADE
The highly specialized A-10 attack aircraft, called "Warthogs" by pilots, were among the most used in the war.

TANK KILLER
To destroy tanks, A-10 attack aircraft use missiles and a huge cannon. It shoots out heavy shells, which are explosives inside cases, at very high speed. During the Gulf War, A-10s destroyed many Iraqi tanks, helping American forces win the war on the ground.

Ammunition drum

Ammunition feed

Chain driven breech

Rotating barrel

21

TRANSPORTERS

World War II proved how useful military transport could be. Since then, specialized transporters have been developed. Transporters have been used in wars and to save hundreds of thousands of lives in disaster areas.

One of the most widely used transport aircraft is the C-130 Hercules. It sits low on the ground and is easy to load using the rear loading ramp. It has a strong undercarriage, a large wing, and powerful engines that enable it to land and take off from short dirt strips. The Hercules can fly at a very steep angle down to a landing without building up too much speed. During the war in Bosnia in the early 1990s, the capital Sarajevo was under siege.

C-130 COCKPIT

C-130 Hercules have been made since 1954. Today, it has a "glass cockpit" full of computer screens to give pilots essential information.

CH-46 Sea Knight

Helicopters are slower, and carry smaller loads than cargo planes. Helicopters do not need runways and can deliver their loads anywhere. The CH-46 Sea Knight helicopter can carry 17 fully equipped soldiers or 15 casualties on stretchers. It has a range of 633 miles (1,020 km), carrying 2,400 lb (1,088 kg).

McDONNELL DOUGLAS C-17

The latest U.S. transporter is the C-17. Like the Hercules, it is used for both military and humanitarian missions. During the war in Afghanistan in 2001, C-17 transporters flew more than 200 humanitarian missions, air dropping more than 2.4 million packages of food and blankets to people in need.

Transport aircraft flew in food and medicine. They were shot at by small arms fire and had to fly a steep approach in order to minimize time spent at low level. Transporters are now sometimes equipped with chaff and flares for protection against missiles.

UNLOADING ON THE MOVE

Loads might be pulled out of a very low-flying aircraft by a single parachute. The Hercules flies slowly using extended flaps on the wings.

HEAVY DROPS

It is best to land to unload a transporter. Supplies dropped from the air by parachute might land in the wrong place or be damaged when they hit the ground. In areas of heavy fighting or disaster areas, dropping the load may be the only option, because there may not be a place to land the aircraft. Transport aircraft can drop very heavy loads such as vehicles, guns, or even tanks.

SEA KING

The Sikorsky S-61 is one of the most widely used search and rescue helicopters. It has been used in the United States, Canada (CH-124), Britain (Sea King), Denmark, Malaysia, Argentina, and many other countries.

Nimrod

The British Nimrod MR2 was developed from the first jet airliner. The Nimrod is a maritime patrol aircraft used for reconnaissance over the sea, to hunt down submarines, and as a search and rescue vehicle. It cannot actually pick up survivors but it can search large areas of sea much faster than helicopters. After finding the survivors, the Nimrod can direct ships and helicopters to the scene. It can also drop survival equipment. The Nimrod can fly for twelve hours without refueling.

SEARCH AND RESCUE

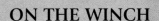

When it comes to helping people in trouble at sea, search and rescue (SAR) helicopters are hard to beat. Even ships may not be able to give help quickly enough. Saving people in howling hurricanes and huge waves is a tough job.

It is dangerous to fly close to a ship being tossed around by the waves. The deck cargo may have been torn loose, or the ship may be on fire, and all this may take place at night at freezing temperatures. To pick up survivors from the sea, it is often necessary to lower the **winch** from the helicopter. On the way down, the person on the winch may crash into waves several feet high. The rescuer may then have to struggle with desperately frightened survivors to bring them up. Some rescuers on winches have been torn from their harnesses and drowned.

ON THE WINCH
The rescuer on the winch is the life-saving link to the helicopter. A complicated rescue operation can last for hours, leaving the rescuer with a difficult question: "Am I too tired to go on?"

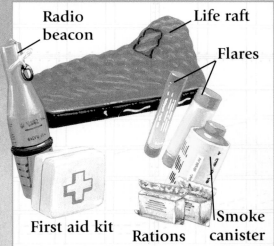

Radio beacon | Life raft | Flares | First aid kit | Rations | Smoke canister

SURVIVAL
Floats and survival kits are carried on board ships. They are also dropped from aircraft. This equipment makes it possible to survive for days at sea – if the kit is not damaged and the survivor can get into the raft. This is not hard to do on a calm sea, but SAR helicopters are called upon to help in more dangerous weather conditions.

SMART PLANES

F-35 JOINT STRIKE FIGHTER
The F-35 fighter jet will be difficult to see on radar, and it can land vertically.

AN EXPENSIVE BOMBER
The B-2 stealth bomber was used over the former Yugoslavia and Afghanistan. Some people have argued that the targets could have been hit by cruise missiles at much lower cost.

The Cold War ended in the 1990s. Since then, many air forces have cut down on their numbers of squadrons and aircraft. Combat aircraft are still in action over places like Iraq, Bosnia, and Kosovo.

Since the end of the Cold War, fighter jets have been used in other combat missions to fight terrorism and to maintain peace. Governments assume military aircraft will be needed in the future, so new types are being developed.

Smart Bombs

A "smart" bomb is a laser-guided bomb that can hit a target very precisely. Smart bombs are expensive but have been used in war in the former Yugoslavia, and the Gulf War. The purpose of these wars was to stop enemies, not to kill large numbers of people. People are still hurt and killed by smart bombs, but they are more accurate than bombs dropped randomly from planes.

A decade is no longer enough time to design a new military aircraft, and they are also very expensive. The Lockheed Martin F-35 Joint Strike Fighter jet will be the future combat aircraft of the U.S. Air Force, Britain's Royal Air Force, and others as well. Not long ago, each air force flew a number of types of aircraft from several different manufacturers. Today, costs are so high that different countries agree on just one type of plane and build it together.

EUROFIGHTER
The Eurofighter will soon be in service with a number of European air forces. It has been almost 20 years since the start of the design of this aircraft.

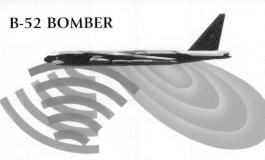

B-52 BOMBER

Strong radar signal

Strong infra red signature

B-2 STEALTH BOMBER

Weak infra red signature

Weak radar signal

CLOAKING
By giving a bomber certain shapes, radar signals are dispersed instead of being sent back, so the radar cannot find the bomber. The hot gases from the exhaust are usually seen using infra red equipment, but the exhaust of the stealth bomber spreads and cools the gases so they leave only a weak signal.

PILOTLESS

Recent air wars over Kosovo and Afghanistan have been fought with few air force casualties. Countries no longer tolerate large numbers of people killed, such as there were in the World Wars.

PHOENIX

The Canadian Phoenix is an unmanned artillery observation aircraft. It can detect targets night and day and transmit the information directly to the command center.

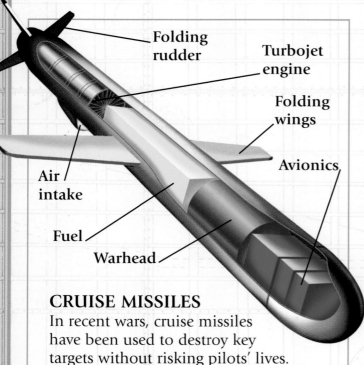

Folding rudder

Turbojet engine

Folding wings

Avionics

Air intake

Fuel

Warhead

CRUISE MISSILES

In recent wars, cruise missiles have been used to destroy key targets without risking pilots' lives. Cruise missiles are small jet aircraft without human pilots that fly to the targets and then explode. Cruise missiles can be launched from aircraft or submarines. Future unmanned combat jets will be remote-controlled and able to perform many more functions than cruise missiles do today.

One way to avoid casualties is to have no pilot in the aircraft. In fact, these aircraft are already in use. During World War I, a pilot usually survived only a couple of weeks doing the job of getting aerial photos of enemy trenches. During the war in Afghanistan in 2001, the U.S. Air Force rushed into service its new remote-controlled RQ-4A Global Hawk. It took photos without risking a pilot's life. Pilotless Combat Air Vehicles (UNCAVs) are now being developed that could carry bombs, missiles, and even nuclear weapons. This has been called "push-button" warfare. In future wars, "pilots" might sit safely on the ground, joy stick in hand, and direct the fighter jets on computer screens. So why not fight the wars 100 percent on computers? It would be cheaper, there would be absolutely no casualties – and the games are already in the stores!

BOEING X-45

The Boeing X-45 is a research aircraft, but it could also be used as a pilotless combat aircraft for destroying enemy air defenses or hitting targets.

Global Hawk

The Global Hawk has a wingspan greater than a World War II bomber, and can fly for 36 hours over the battlefield, taking pictures day or night from high altitude. Its amazingly long range was shown in April 2001 when the Global Hawk became the first pilotless aircraft to fly non-stop across the Pacific from the United States to Australia.

SPOTTERS' GUIDE

Almost all the high-performance military aircraft that have been designed since World War II have been jets. Even a helicopter like the S-61 is powered by two turbine (jet) engines. These engines allow military aircraft to fly much more quickly, and because they use less fuel, modern-day airplanes can fly much further, too.

LOCKHEED SR-71 (BLACKBIRD)
Country: USA
Description: long-range strategic reconnaissance aircraft
Length: 107 ft 5 in (37.7 m)
Wingspan: 55 ft 7 in (16.9 m)
Speed: 2,190 mph (3,530 km/h)

BELL X-1
Country: USA
Description: experimental rocket plane
Length: 30 ft 11 in (9.4 m)
Wingspan: 28 ft (8.5 m)
Speed: 1,650 mph (2,640 km/h)

MIKOYAN-GUREVICH MiG-15
Country: USSR
Description: single seat fighter
Length: 33 ft (10 m)
Wingspan: 33 ft (10 m)
Speed: 652 mph (1,050 km/h)

NORTH AMERICAN F-86 SABRE
Country: USA
Description: interceptor and fighter bomber
Length: 37 ft 6 in (11.4 m)
Wingspan: 39 ft 1 in (11.9 m)
Speed: 678 mph (1,091 km/h)

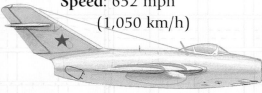

BRITISH AEROSPACE HARRIER
Country: Britain
Description: single seater fighter and reconnaissance aircraft
Length: 45 ft 6 in (13.9 m)
Wingspan: 25 ft 3 in (7.7 m)
Speed: 720 mph (1,160 km/h)

BOEING B-52 STRATOFORTRESS
Country: USA
Description: long-range strategic bomber
Length: 157 ft 7 in (48 m)
Wingspan: 185 ft (56.4 m)
Speed: 650 mph (1,040 km/h)

PANAVIA TORNADO

Country: Britain, Germany, and Italy
Description: two seat multi-role fighter bomber
Length: 59 ft 3 in (18 m)
Wingspan: 45 ft 7 in (13.9 m) (wings extended)
27 ft (8.6 m) (wings folded)
Speed: 1,450 mph (2,333 km/h)

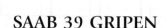

SAAB 39 GRIPEN

Country: Sweden
Description: multi-role fighter
Length: 45 ft 11 in (14 m)
Wingspan: 26 ft 3 in (8 m)
Speed: 1,320 mph (2,135 km/h)

SIKORSKY S-61B SEA KING

Country: USA
Description: anti-submarine, air-sea rescue, and transport helicopter
Length: 46 ft 9 in (14.3 m)
Rotor diameter: 56 ft (17 m)
Speed: 123 mph (198 km/h)

FAIRCHILD REPUBLIC A-10 THUNDERBOLT (WARTHOG)

Country: USA
Description: close support attack aircraft
Length: 53 ft 4 in (16.3 m)
Wingspan: 57 ft 6 in (17.5 m)
Speed: 423 mph (681 km/h)

NORTHROP B-2 STEALTH BOMBER

Country: USA
Description: two seater bomber
Length: 69 ft (20.9 m)
Wingspan: 172 ft (52.4 m)
Speed: 475 mph (764 km/h)

INDEX

GLOSSARY

AERODYNAMICS The study of how objects move through air.

COMMUNIST The belief in communism, or that all wealth should be in the hands of the government.

DEMOCRATIC The system in which people govern through elected representatives.

JET ENGINE An engine that causes forward motion by forcing hot gases from a rear opening.

HOMING IN To be guided to a target automatically.

HUMANITARIAN To help people who are suffering.

MISSION A combat operation assigned to a person or group.

NUCLEAR BOMB A bomb with great explosive power.

PISTON ENGINE A circular disk that moves back and forth in a cylinder. In engines, pistons are moved by igniting fuel and air.

RADAR WARNING RECEIVER A device in an aircraft that warns if an enemy is trying to catch it.

RECONNAISSANCE The inspection of an area to gather information.

ROCKET POWERED A vehicle powered by a rocket engine, in which an explosion in the engine forces the vehicle to move ahead very quickly.

SORTIE A military flight by a single aircraft.

STRAFE An attack with bullets and bombs from a low-flying aircraft.

SUPERSONIC Faster than the speed of sound.

TANKER A ship, truck, or aircraft that has tanks for carrying liquid.

TERRORISTS People who try to achieve goals using violence.

TRANSPORT AIRCRAFT An aircraft designed especially for carrying people or freight.

WINCH A machine for pulling or lifting heavy objects.